FOREX FOR BEGINNERS

Proven Step by Step Strategies for Making Money in Forex Trading

Mark Smith

The information herein is offered for informational purposes solely, and is universal as so. The presentation of the information is without contract or any type of guarantee assurance.

The trademarks that are used are without any consent, and the publication of the trademark is without permission or backing by the trademark owner. All trademarks and brands within this book are for clarifying purposes only and are the owned by the owners themselves, not affiliated with this document.

Table of Contents

Introduction

I want to thank you and congratulate you for purchasing the book, *"Forex for Beginners: Proven Step-by-Step Strategies for Making Money in Forex Trading"*.

This book contains proven steps and strategies on the workings of the forex markets, the basic terminology involved, and ways and methods to make money in forex trading. Let's start at the very beginning.

What is Forex and what are Forex Markets?

Forex, or foreign exchange, deals with currencies of various countries. Forex markets are platforms wherein banks, governments, businesses, traders, and investors meet to buy and sell foreign exchange or forex for short. Forex markets are open for business 5 days a week and 24 hours a day. Important forex markets are located in New York, London, Zurich, Tokyo, Hong Kong, Frankfurt, Sydney, Singapore, and Paris.

How did the Forex begin?

Back in 1876, the gold standard system was set up which made it mandatory for all nations to back their currencies with solid gold. This meant that the value of the currency was directly linked to that of gold. This system was called Bretton Woods monetary system.

In 1971, the United States of America stopped using this system and adopted fiat money instead. In "fiat money" system, the government declared the currency as legal tender and it does not need the backing of physical gold or silver. The value of the currency is arrived at by the relationship between the demand and supply of the currency.

Today, no government follows the gold standard system and all of them follow the fiat money system. The term "fiat" means an order. Hence fiat money translates to the currency, which the government "orders" to accept as a form of payment or legal tender. Fiat money is not backed by any physical commodity such as gold or silver; it is based only on faith. The fall of the Bretton Woods system marked the beginning of floating currency rates and thus the concept of foreign exchange markets was born.

What is forex trading? Why is it so popular?

Forex trading involves trading in currency pairs. For instance, if you believe that the rate of USD is going to rise against that of EUR, then you would like to buy the USD/EUR pair at a low price and then sell it when it goes up as per your expectations. However, please remember that if the USD rates fell, then you would make a loss. So it is imperative to be aware of risks involved in forex trading before plunging into it.

The popularity of forex trading is directly linked to the immense earnings potential it has for you. It is necessary for you to know that while trading in foreign exchange does involve speculation, if you maintain a disciplined and knowledge-based approach, you can make a decent amount of money in this place.

Here are some basic tips and skills that you need to develop if you want to do well in forex trading:

- **Emotional quotient has to be robust** – do not be overwhelmed by losses. You have to build the strength to accept losses with equanimity.

- **Fearlessness and confidence** – be confident in yourself and your working strategy. Be fearless when it comes to taking calculated risks.

- **Discipline, dedication, focus and self-control** – do not waver in your strategy and give in to market temptations. Stick to and focus on your well-planned and well-thought-out strategy.

- **Objective outlook** – see the market with an unemotional and non-subjective perspective. Keep profits as your only goal.

- **Realistic approach** – remember not to treat the forex market as a magic wand or a lottery that will make you rich overnight. It requires you to be patient, hardworking, committed, and diligent to achieve set monetary targets.

- **Savvy** – be knowledge-savvy and tech-savvy. Imbibe data like a sponge and leverage your learning to make profits. Keep updating yourself with the latest information and data.

You must build skills to learn and master the art of making money on the forex markets by taking advantage of volatility in the market and strictly following your set strategy.

The retail forex trading market (meant for individual investors like you and me) is a growing market as more and more people are attracted by the potential profits that this place can yield.

Moreover, today's advanced technology has made it easy for individuals to access and participate in these markets.

There are two kinds of intermediaries who can help us participate in the forex market:

- Dealers – are also known as "market makers" because they "make the market" for you. They act as counterparties for you and quote a price that they will do the transaction at. Dealers make their money on the spread or the difference between the buying and selling price.
- Brokers – are agents who find the best price available in the market for you. They make their money through a commission they charge that is over and above the transaction cost.

There are multiple advantages in forex trading and here a couple of them that I hope will entice you to make an entry to this highly potential arena:

Largest market – Trading volumes on a daily basis is over $3 trillion giving you ample surface area to enter and exit at strategic times and places increasing your chances to make money.

- No closing hours – you can trade whenever you want
- Easily accessible – A small amount, as small as $250, is sufficient to start a forex trading account. Many brokers allow you to start trading the same day you open your account and moreover, online options allow you to trade vide the click of a mouse.
- No geographical boundaries – you can trade in the confines of your home with just a computer and Internet connection.

At this juncture, it would be prudent to use a word of caution, especially for beginners. While there is immense potential to make money through forex trading, remember that it does carry risk, too. Entering the forex markets without being thoroughly aware of risk is not just imprudent but also extremely foolhardy. You must be aware that if there is the high potential for making profits, there also exists ample potential for losses.

Chapter 1: Jargon in Forex Trading

While there are many currencies in the world, the ones that are commonly traded in the forex markets along with their mnemonics are:

- US Dollar – USD
- Euro – EUR
- Japanese Yen – JPY
- British Pounds – GBP
- Swiss Franc – CHF
- Canadian Dollar – CAD
- Australian Dollar – AUD
- New Zealand Dollar – NZD

The forex market uses its own set of jargon and before you enter the market to start making money you have to know them really well. Some basic terms that are commonly used include:

Currency pairs – In the forex markets, rates are always quoted using currency pairs. This is because you are buying one currency by paying for it in the other currency.

Exchange rate – is the value of one currency expressed in relation to another. For instance, if the buy exchange rate of EUR/USD is 1.35 then it means that you will have to pay 1.35 USD to buy 1 EUR; if the sell exchange rate of EUR/USD is 1.35 then it means you will receive 1.35 USD for 1 EUR.

Base currency and quote currency – In forex trading, you are selling one currency to buy another currency. If the currency pair EUR/USD is quoted at 1.35 in a trade, it means you are buying 1.35USD for 1 EUR. Here, EUR is called the base currency and USD is called the quote currency.

An easy way to remember the concept of base and quote currency is that the BASE currency is the BASIS on which the trade is happening. Again for example, if you are selling EUR/USD, then it means you are selling the base currency (the first of the pair) to buy USD (the second of the pair); and if you are buying EUR/USD, then it means that you are buying the base currency (EUR) and selling the quote currency (USD).

Long position – Long position means you are purchasing the base currency and selling the quote currency. It means that you are buying it hoping the price of the base currency will rise.

Short position – Short position means you are selling the base currency and purchasing the quote currency. It means that you are selling it hoping that the price of the base currency will fall.

Cross-rate – is the exchange rate between two currencies neither of which is the currency of the country where the exchange rate is quoted. For instance, if EUR/YEN exchange rate is quoted in the US, then it is referred to as cross-rate as neither EUR nor YEN is the official currency in the US.

Pip – stands for "price interest point." It is the smallest change in price movement that a currency pair can make. It is sometimes referred to as point or points. For instance, 1 pip for EUR/USD is 0.0001. For a currency pair where one of them is JPY, the pip is 0.01.

Margin – This is the money deposited with your broker to trade in foreign exchange. The amount of money deposited by you in terms of the percentage of the actual forex trading transaction cost is called margin deposit that is held in a margin account. Margin accounts are opened and maintained by brokers and dealers.

Leverage – Leverage is the capacity to use a small amount to participate in large transactions. Leverage is the ratio of the amount of transaction to the actual investment. This enables you to trade with only a percentage of the transaction size. It is a loan given to you by your broker through your margin account to trade in forex.

The issue with leverage is that while you can make a considerable amount of money by investing a small amount initially, there is ample potential for you to incur large losses too. The success of trading in leverage depends on your own trading skills, knowledge of the forex market, and your risk management skills

A 50:1 leverage means for every $1 you have in your margin account, you can place or order a transaction worth $50. Similarly, a 100:1 leverage means you can transact for $100 for every $1 that you have in your account. These ratios are set by the brokers as per their own policy. When you open your account with them, you have to clarify what leverage options they offer.

Ask price – Ask price is the rate at which your broker is willing to sell you the base currency in return for quote currency.

Bid price – Bid price is the rate at which your broker is willing to buy the base currency from you to give you quote currency.

Spread – The difference between the ask price and the bid price is called the spread.

Support and Release Levels – are the price levels or price points that usually currencies do not go under (support) or go over (resistance). Analyzing and knowing these levels will help you choose the best available time for opening and closing trades. However, you must remember that these support and resistance levels are by no means concrete or fixed and is as fluid as ever. Yet, with experience and increased technical know-how, you will gain ample skills to identify and spot these levels in order to use them to your advantage.

Pivot points – These are indicators integrated into most forex customer support platforms. These indicators will reflect previous highs and lows of the currency in question.

Trend trading – This kind of trading is probably the best to start your trading experience in since the market is moving in a single general direction. It, therefore, makes sense to enter the market in this direction to result in a profitable trade. These trends, however, do end at some point and you must be aware that you are running the risk of entering perhaps towards the end-point and hence could be heading to a potential loss. This skill is also one that requires a practiced eye and continuous learning.

Counter-trend trading – As the name suggests, this kind of trading entails entering the market at the point where the trend trading is expected to reverse. This type is definitely riskier than trend trading and you should opt for this only when you are convinced of your mastery in the forex market.

Trading Edge – In any trading market, having a trading edge means collating a set of conditions which when it occurs has a much higher chance of working well for you than not working. In forex trading too, you must be able to arrive at what your optimum trading edge. This can be achieved through learning, analyzing, and watching and keeping track of the market. The keenly discerning eye will, of course, need lots of patience and hard work

Once you understand the basic terminology in use at the markets, you can move ahead, open your account and start trading in foreign exchange and with patience, diligence, hard work, and discipline begin to make money.

Chapter 2: Order Types

To make money in forex trading one of the most important things to know and understand what kinds of order types exist and which order type to choose, depending on whether the market or falling. There is no concept of bullish or bearish market conditions as in trading stocks. There is potential to make money in both kinds of situations in forex trading.

Before we go to order types, I would like to reiterate the concept of buying and selling and go into more detail on long and short selling.

Concept of buying and selling in forex trading

The most basic concept of making money in forex trading is to sell high/buy low and buy low/sell high. The latter part is quite clear, meaning to say, you buy the currency at a lower price and sell at a higher price and the difference is your profit. However, the former part may sound a little confounding for many beginners. The foremost question is how do I sell something I do not have at all, in the first place? This will be covered in long and short positions.

The logic of trading in forex is based on the currency pair. If you are involved in the sell transaction of a currency pair, you are actually selling the base currency to buy the quote currency (remember definitions of basic terminology in Chapter 2). And when you are involved in the buy transaction of a currency pair, you are buying the base currency in exchange for quote currency.

Long and short selling

Long selling – means we are buying into the market and hence want the market to go up so that we can sell at a higher price than we bought at to make some profit. This also means we are buying the first (base) currency and selling the second quoteocurrency of a currency pair. Hence, for the sake of an example, if you buy EUR/USD and the EUR becomes stronger than USD, then your transaction is profitable for you.

Short selling – means you are selling the market and hence you want it to fall. When the market falls you can buy back the currency at a lower price and the difference between the price you sold at and the lower price you bought at will again become your profit. So to explain with an example, if you sold GBP/USD and the GBP became weaker against the USD, your transaction is profitable for you.

Order Types

Now it is time to understand the order types that are available to you in the forex market. When you execute a trading transaction in the market, it is called an "order." The following types are usually available with most brokers:

Market order – is executed immediately on receipt by the broker at the market's best available price

Limit Entry Order – is placed to either buy below the market or sell above the market. An example is given here for better understanding – if the EUR/USD is being quoted at 1.335 and you want to sell when it reaches 1.435, then you place a limit sell order with your broker. So, when the market reaches this position, it will make up your short position and leave you in a profitable transaction. If you wish to buy at 1.325

when the market is trading at 1.335, then when the market reaches your desired price, then you will be able to make up your long position.

Stop Loss Order – as the name suggests, this kind of order is meant to be used if you do not want to increase your losses. Stop loss orders help you control your profits and/or losses.

Stop Entry Order – is used if you want to sell below the current market price or buy above the market price. The difference between Limit Entry Order and Stop Entry order is the former is designed to enter the market at favorable prices whereas the latter helps you enter the market at less agreeable conditions.

Trailing Stop Order – this works similar to stop-loss order except that it trails the market price at a distance that is specified by you in the order. For example, if you set up a 50 pip trailing stop order for EUR/USD, the order will not be executed until your position is favorable by 51 pips. Again, the trading will stop till another 51 pips in your favor occurs. This allows you to book profits while your order continues to be executed as per your instructions.

Good for the Day Order (GFD) – This order remains active in the market until the end of the day. As we are dealing with a 24-hour working condition, please check with your broker as to the 'day' that he works with. It could vary from dealer to dealer.

Good till Cancelled Order (GTC) - Meaning exactly what the name says, this order type will remain in effect till you choose to manually annul it. The flip side of this order type is that you could place the order and then erroneously forget about it. This could lead to a potentially unfavorable market condition when this order gets executed and you could then incur losses.

Once you know and understand how these order types work, you can leverage the advantage of each type depending on the kind of transaction you are doing.

Chapter 3: How to Calculate Your Profits and Losses?

In order to learn to calculate your profits and losses, you need to know the following:
- What are lot/lot size
- Calculate pip value
- Then calculate profit/loss

Lot/lot size

Positions are calculated based on "lots." The commonly used lots are classified and known as:
- Standard lot – with 100, 000 units
- Mini lot – with 10,000 units
- Micro lot – with 1000 units
- Nano lot – with 100 units

How to arrive at pip value

You already know that pip (price interest point) is the smallest price increment of any currency in the market. In order that you make a significant amount of money from these small changes, you need to trade in large amounts in the currency of your choice. Leverage is what will be of help to you for transacting in large amounts (see chapter 2 on "Jargon in Forex Trading to recollect what leverage means). The following examples will help you understand how lot size and pip value are related.

Example 1: To calculate the pip value of one standard lot of EUR/JPY quoted at 100.50, the formula is 0.01 (as this is the pip for any JPY currency pair) divided by 100.50 multiplied by 100,000 (units in a standard lot). So the required pip value would be:

0.01/100.50×100,000 = $9.95

Example 2: To calculate the pip value of one standard lot of USD/CHF quoted at 0.9190, the formula is 0.0001 (as this is the pip for USD/CHF currency pair) divided by 0.9190 multiplied by 100,000 (units in a standard lot). So the required pip value would be:

0.0001/0.9190×100,000 = $10.88

In currency pairs wherein USD is the quote currency, then the pip value of one standard lot will always be equal of $10; the pip value of one mini lot will be equal to $1; the pip value of one micro lot will be equal to $0.1; the pip value of one nano lot will be $0.01.

How to calculate your profits and/or losses

Let us use examples to learn how to arrive at profits and losses.

Example 1: The rate of USD/CHF is 0.9191/0.9195. If you want to sell USD/CHF then you will have to use the bid price of 0.9191, which is the rate that the market will purchase USD from you.

You decide to sell one standard lot (100,000 units) at $0.9191

After two days, the quote for USD/CHF is 0.9091/0.9095. Now you wish to close this trade and take your profits.

20

For this, you must now look at the ask price as you are now buying USD/CHF since you initially sold the USD/CHF. The new ask price is 0.9095. The difference between what you first sold at (0.9191) and what you now buy at (0.9095) is 0.0096 or 96 pips.

Using the same formula used to calculate the pip value, the value of one pip at the quoted price will be as follows: 0.0001/0.9095×100,000 = $10.99 per pip

So the value of 96 pips is $10.99×96 = $1,055.04. This is the profit you made in the above example.

Example 2: For currency pairs where USD is the quote currency, you simply need to multiply the gain or loss of pips with the dollar value per pip.

Suppose you buy EUR/USD at 1.3200 but the price has fallen to 1.3100. That means you have lost 100 pips. So if you were trading 100,000 units (a standard lot, your loss would be $10 (the dollar value of one standard lot when the quote currency is USD) multiplied by the number of pips lost. In this example, you lose $10×100 (pips lost), which is equal to $1000.

If the transaction was done in one mini lot (10,000 units) your loss would be $1 (the dollar value of one mini lot when the quote currency is USD) multiplied by the number of pips lost. Here, you stand to lose $1×100 (pips lost), which is equal to $100.

A key learning to remember when you are calculating profit/loss in forex is to use the correct exchange rate. You must use bid price when you are selling and the ask price when you are buying. This spread between the bid and ask price is crucial is calculating the correct value of profits and/or losses.

Chapter 4: Forex Trading Plans

To become a successful forex trader, planning and strategizing is critical. There are umpteen failure stories that are based on either the lack of planning and/or not adhering to the set strategy/plan. It is critical that as a novice, you pick up the correct habit of doing both things; setting up a strong plan and strictly adhering to it even in seemingly tempting and violent market conditions.

There are a couple of things that you need to do to maintain discipline and an organized attitude in forex trading.
- Make a forex trading plan
- Keep a forex trading journal
- Update and maintain relevancy of the above two aspects without fail

Trading plans should have a set routine – If this routine is absent, then you will not know when, where, and how to give or cancel orders. The routine brings in a sense of discipline to your work ethics.

A good analogy to working successfully in forex markets would be the operational mind of a sniper. A good sniper is patient, disciplined, and diligently waiting quietly for his "easy prey." As a forex trader, the easiest prey for you would be the most obviously seen trade setups.

Checklists

You should include a checklist in your trading plans. This checklist should have items that you will look for in the forex market before you placing an order. If all the items are ticked in your checklist, only then should you go ahead with the order. Even if one item is missing a tick, then hold off the trade.

Written Guidelines

Your trading strategy should definitely include a detailed description of your actions in the market. Some of the things to include in the written guidelines are:

- Your trading edge
- How you will trade it
- When you will trade it
- Your preferred time frames to trade
- Your risk management strategy
- Your profit taking strategy
- Your overall goals
- Images of trading setups

Once you have written down the guidelines, keep updating it with new skills and knowledge that you have picked up on your journey. The image of your trading setup should become an imprint in your head such that you can recover it and know if the current market setup matches yours.

Keep Records of all Transactions

Keep a trading journal and record all your transactions (both loss- and profit-incurred transactions) diligently and without fail. This journal is a great way to keep you grounded when you think you are flying too high because of a few successes or feeling too depressed because of a few failures. Moreover, regularly checking your journal gives you feedback on your own performances and learning gets better.

Plan trades in Advance in "Anticipation" of results

Perhaps the most important aspect of planning ahead before actual trading is that being outside the market gives you an objective overview of possible situations and expected outcomes. This keeps your working process free from subjective perspectives that can arise when you are actually participating in the market. This "planning in advance" also keeps out unnecessary and undue market influences that have the potential to hurt your success. Prolonged practice at this will make you less of an "emotional" trader and hence outcomes will be more likely to be profitable than otherwise.

Patience

Unlike in stock trading where you invest and wait patiently for the right price to sell, here patience is more associated with waiting for the trading edge most suitable for you as per the strategy you have already arrived at. This kind of patient trading will result in more positive outcomes than those that take place because of emotional calls or due to not having the patience to wait out for the correct market position.

It is common knowledge that traders who do not exhibit patience to wait for the ideal trading setup are far more likely to lose money than those who wait. This patience has to be a critical factor in your trading plan and descriptive guideline. Thus, every time you read your notes, you will be reminded of the criticality of patience.

Chapter 5: Forex Brokers

What Forex Brokers Do?

Forex brokers provide investors and traders with the means to trade currencies and some other financial instruments. That includes pro- viding liquidity, leverage, software, support, etc.

What Types of Forex Brokers Are There?

There are two general types of retail Forex brokers:

• Dealing Desk Brokers, also called Market Makers. provide liquidity to the market by offering both buy and sell quotes (Bid and Ask) and taking the other side of the trade. That is the reason they are also called Market Makers. Dealing desk brokers do not charge commissions for trading. They add commissions to the spread in the form of extra pips added to the interbank quote (see also What Is A Spread? and What Is A Pip?).

• No Dealing Desk Brokers. There are two types of No Dealing Desk Brokers:

• Straight Through Processors (STP) - brokers who connect traders with the interbank market. They collect quotes from multiple sources and present the trader with the best bid and ask prices adding some pips as their commission.

• Electronic Communications Networks (ECN) – brokers that allow direct trading between all participants of their network. They do not alter the spreads and charge small commissions for each trade. The true ECN model eliminates conflict of interest that exists when brokers take the opposite side of the trade.

How to Choose A Forex Broker?

Not all brokers are created equal and one has to do a bit of re-search before committing any funds. The following is a list of things to check before opening an account:

1. We recommend dealing only reputable regulated brokers.

2. Make sure to open the right account type. If you are a beginner you must choose a micro-lot account type maybe a mini-lot and Not a standard-lot. Prefer a demo account to start with.

3. Be careful when using capital leverage. High leverage does not just increase your trading risk but your trading cost too.

4. Be careful with the spread you pay on each currency pair (popular currencies such is EURUSD or GBPUSD are traded less expensive than less popular currencies such is USDTRY)

5. Make sure to place always a stop-loss

6. Be careful where you place your stop-loss orders (Do not place the stop-loss too close)

7. Be careful when trading intraday, only a few traders can beat the market intraday

8. Understand that you are a little fish swimming in oceanic waters with many sharks. Protect your capital. The secret when trading in any Financial market is to protect your capital and not become rich in no-time (keep that always in mind)

Chapter 6: Common Mistakes and How to Avoid Them

The best of forex traders have not been spared by some common mistakes and traps that the market holds in store. Being aware of these traps is a great way to ensure that you can handle them well when you encounter them. Here are some common errors and market traps that can pull the carpet from under your feet:

Over-analysis

More is better is not really true for making a success of your forex trading endeavors. Most of the important points that are needed to make an effective trading strategy are available through the price action chart. Use these critical points and make a robust trading plan that suits your temperament and risk management capabilities. Sifting through tons of data from innumerable Forex-based news can hurt you more than help you. Keep your trading charts as minimalistic as possible without overcrowding it with data from anywhere and yet ensuring that critical things are not left out.

Excessive trading

Many failures in the forex markets are due to over-trading. Most traders who do not make money are those who over-trade in the markets. A strange thing about trading in forex is that most people make a lot of money when they use demo accounts; however, they are not able to replicate this success in real-time trading.

This is because in demo trading there is absolutely no emotion whereas in real-time trading since your money is in the line, invariably, emotions creep their way into your psyche and cause trouble. Hence, it is important to remember emotions in trading will not deliver success. Only an objective and clear-thinking strategy will help. Over-trading people are more often not basing their decisions on emotions.

The following instances will help you realize if and when you are trading excessively which will, hopefully, put you on guard:

- Executing orders when your pre-determined trading edges as per your strategy plan are not reached
- Not having a clearly defined trading plan

Hence, preventing excessive trading bouts is possible if your trading plans are perfectly planned and executed. Such a situation will ensure that you execute only those orders that have a better chance of success than otherwise.

Risk Management

Being fully aware of your own risk potential and managing your money to reflect this aspect is a key element for success in forex trading. If you realize and accept the fact that you could lose the money you have invested translates to being open to losses as per your risk appetite. Risking amounts beyond your risk appetite is clearly imprudent and can lead to potentially large and irrecoverable losses, not to mention, denting your own confidence levels.

Become a master at demo trading before plunging into live scenarios

It is extremely important to keep working out trading scenarios in demo/practice accounts and master techniques before you jump into real trading. Using demo accounts effectively will help you learn techniques and arrive at strategies that match your needs and risk profile. On the flip side, depending too much on demo trading can make you a little too "emotion-less" and when you actually dive into real trading, the emotional aspect might hit you harder than you'd like.

Hence, after mastering techniques and getting some amount of success in demo trading, it makes sense to get into live scenarios. Moreover, when you start live trading, remember to begin with small amounts; gain confidence slowly but surely and only then increase stakes in small batches.

Find a good, reputable, and dependable broker

The forex markets are far riskier than other markets and hence are filled with not-so-good brokers who can deliver you more harm than good. Please ensure that you open a forex trading account only with brokers who hold approved licenses from appropriate authorities.

Know all the offers that your trading/margin account is privy to including leverage amounts, charges/commissions, account funding and withdrawal policies, and spread-related information. A good customer service attitude is a trademark of any good broker; make sure this aspect is clearly visible before you sign on the dotted line.

Employ leverage amounts sensibly

Remember leverage is a loan given to you by your broker and no matter how attractive it sounds, if you lose money in the transaction then you need to cover the lost amount from your pocket. So while leverage is a great way to increase your potential to make money by investing a small percentage, it also can enhance the potential for making losses. Hence use leverages sensibly and keeping in mind your risk appetite.

Being aware of loopholes, traps, and common mistakes that occur in forex trading is an important aspect of enhancing your chances to make money. Spend a little bit of time knowing and learning about these mistakes and how to avoid them.

Conclusion

While the foreign markets give you ample opportunities to make money and it is unwise not to take advantage of such opportunities, it would be imprudent to take a plunge without picking up and mastering the requisite skills. Starting from the basics and going into complex yet potentially profitable transactions require time, patience, and oodles of hard work and diligence from your end.

However, once you have mastered the techniques in forex trading, the amount of money you can make has no limits. The world is replete with such success stories. But I would like to reiterate the importance of prudence and patience to achieving this kind of success.

Know yourself well, know the markets well and then match what the market has to offer with what you can and will make an effort to take. You are sure to succeed. Remember to treat forex trading as a business that requires objective thinking and some seemingly difficult decisions. Just like in any business, short term losses and profits are not as important as the discipline and dedication you bring to the table that will yield far more sustainable and long-term returns.

It is important to keep in mind that just like how small businesses do not become overnight successes, similarly forex trading cannot and will not give you overnight success. Endeavor and you shall definitely see success. Do not be overwhelmed and hence get carried away by short terms successes and failures.

Thank you again for purchasing this book!

I hope this book was able to help you to get a good understanding of how the forex markets work and how you can leverage the advantages to making money.

The next step is to find a good dealer, start and work on a practice account, and then get into the real world trading slowly but surely. Remember to start small and work gradually towards BIG!

Thank you and good luck!

www.ingramcontent.com/pod-product-compliance
Lightning Source LLC
Chambersburg PA
CBHW071533210326
41597CB00018B/2983